When Deadly Creatures Fight - Who Would Win

Brian Good

ISBN-13: 9781484160244

GREY WHALE PUBLISHING

For more great books visit
www.greywhalepublishing.com

Contents

Introduction

Over many thousands of years some truly fearsome creatures have evolved. From the big cats armed with razor sharp talons, and teeth capable of tearing through the toughest hide, through highly venomous reptiles, snakes and insects, to the giant and ferocious creatures swimming in our oceans. Each is a master of its own realm, and each will attack relentlessly if it feels threatened.

But, if nature were to throw these creatures together into a battle arena to face-up to one another, just who would win?

This book does just that. It pits predator against deadly predator, examines their strengths and weaknesses, looks at real matches that have been fought throughout history, and reveals in detail, When deadly creatures fight - who would win.

The battle lines are drawn between ten pairs of terrifying killing machines:

- The mighty Lion versus the ferocious Grizzly Bear
- The Tarantula versus the Scorpion
- The Crocodile versus the Alligator
- The Rhinoceros versus the African Elephant
- The Hippopotamus versus the Crocodile
- The Eagle versus the Vulture
- The Killer Whale versus the Great White Shark
- The Grey Wolf versus the Spotted Hyena
- The Polar Bear versus the Kodiak Bear
- The Lion versus the Tiger

Let's get things underway and go straight to our first bout. Two giants of the sea, each a terrifying killer, each capable of winning a fight to the death.

So just who would win a battle between a Killer Whale and a Great White Shark...

Killer Whale V's Great White Shark

Deep Sea Duel

Have you ever wondered who would win a fight between a killer whale and a great white shark? Both of them are big, intimidating animals that have stamina, speed and a killer reputation. On one hand, you have the great white shark, one of the most feared creatures in the world. But, the killer whale has quite a reputation too; they don't call it a killer whale for nothing.

Check out these fun facts on these two sea creatures:

Killer whale: Killer whales get their name for a very good reason: They kill. A typical female killer whale grows quite big, weighing in 16,000 lbs and measuring in at a whopping 28 feet in length. Male killer whales grow approximately 32 feet in length and weigh 22,000 to 24,000 pounds.

FACT

Killer Whales are really dolphins. They are the largest dolphins in existence, and can be up to 30 foot long.

They eat and kill all types of animals, including dolphins, whales and sharks. Speed and strength are the two most important killing advantages these animals have. On average, killer whales, also known as Orca's, can reach speeds of 30 mph, thus making them one of the fastest animals in the sea.

Oh, let's not forget the fact that these creatures are
chain, which means they don't have to worry
anything, including sharks. Did you know that kill
fiercest predator? Well, it's true.

Great white shark: Big, strong and fast, great w
animal in the sea. When this sea creature opens it. _
row upon row of sharp teeth. A typical great white shark has aroun.
teeth in its mouth. These sharks are believed to be at the top of the food
chain, and they feast on a wide array of animals from sea turtles to seals. Its
sense of smell helps the great white find food, and they can actually smell a
single drop of blood from miles away.

FACT

If you put a shark into a
swimming pool,
it would be able to smell
a single drop of blood in
the water.

Who would win a fight? Well, both these animals have their strengths. Both
are quick, strong and fierce. But, the winner of a fight would be the... killer
whale.

Why would the killer whale win? Well, although sharks have super sharp
teeth, killer whales are larger and smarter. In a fight, a killer whale would
flip the shark upside down, which is a position where the shark is helpless
and can't fight back. Then, the whale would use its own sharp teeth to kill
the shark. In fact, the only two predators a great white has to worry about
are humans and killer whales. Who knew?

Scorpion V's Tarantula

A Venomous Rivalry

Tarantulas and scorpions are a lot alike: they are similar in size, they both have venom, and they both are at the top of the food chain. Since they are both high up in the food chain, they rarely fight head-to-head. However, that doesn't mean that fights don't occur. Who do you think would win a battle? A scorpion or a tarantula?

Tarantula: The tarantula is a large spider that usually gets a bad reputation. Although they are portrayed as blood-thirsty killers in movies and books, the truth is, they are actually afraid of humans. Nevertheless, these spiders are feared in the animal kingdom for their sneak attacks.

FACT
Spiders are not insects, they are arachnids. Spiders have 8 legs while insects have 6.

To catch their next meal, these spiders hide in burrows in the ground and wait for the prey to come around. Once the prey is in short proximity, the tarantula would sneak-attack it and inject its potent venom. The tarantula's venom would instantly paralyze the prey.

Tarantulas eat a lot of different animals in their diet. Lizards, small frogs, other spiders, small insects, baby snakes and even small birds are among the list of potential prey for this stealthy killer.

To defend itself from attackers, the tarantula would resort to two things: to run away or to inject its potent venom. Tarantulas, however, have a difficult time hunting or fighting when they don't have the element of surprise to their advantage.

FACT
Scorpions do not have bones instead they have an exoskeleton made of chitin, the same thing our fingernails are made of.

Scorpions: Scorpions are mostly dessert creatures that live in multiple locations worldwide, from the tropical rainforest, to the African desserts, to the Australian outback. These creatures range in size from smaller ones to the large, intimidating 7 inch ones. The scorpion's main defense mechanism, which also helps it gather food, is its stinger. Every species of scorpion has a stinger with venom. When a scorpion is defending itself or hunting food, it will inject its venom, instantly killing its victim. But don't worry, a scorpion's venom isn't potent enough to kill a human.

Who would win a fight between a scorpion and a tarantula? That's a tough call, and it really depends on the fight. In a fair fight, which means that the tarantula wouldn't be in its natural habitat, a scorpion would definitely win. Since tarantulas depend on sneak attacks, they rarely fight head-to-head, giving the scorpion the upper hand. However, if the tarantula would have its advantage, meaning it would be hidden in its burrow, it would win. In terms of strength, stamina and venom, a scorpion would win a head-to-head battle, thanks to its potent venom and tough exterior armor.

Strangely, if you were to introduce a seemingly gentle centipede into the battle, it would easily defeat both the tarantula and the scorpion! Weird eh?

Grey Wolf V's Spotted H

Howling Hostility

In a contest between a grey wolf and a spotted hyena, the hyena win every time. It wouldn't even be close. Now, I've never heard of a hyena and a grey wolf fighting and it would take quite a mean person to put them in a cage and let them have at it, but this is why the hyena would win:

FACT

Wolf pups are born deaf and blind.
They begin to see only after 9 to 12 days

If nothing else, the wolf can't match the hyena for the sheer power of its jaws and teeth. The hyena's jaws can crunch down with a pressure of 11,400 pounds per square inch. The spotted hyena is from sub-Saharan Africa and many of the animals it feeds upon are large and have dense bones. Also, the hyena's competitors for this prey include lions, leopards

ild dogs, all of whom are fairly formidable. Hyenas have also been
wn to attack these competitors, though, of course, lions and leopards
e quite capable of killing hyenas.

By contrast, the grey wolf's jaws can only deliver 1,500 pounds per square
inch of pressure. It's also a smaller and less robust animal. An adult male
grey wolf is a little over five feet long, stands about 34 inches high at the
shoulder and weighs up to 85 pounds. An adult spotted hyena female is a
bit longer, stands about 36 inches high at the shoulder and can weigh over
150 pounds. By the way, female hyenas are bigger than males and the
spotted hyena society is matriarchal, which means that the females rule.

Hyenas and wolves can run about as fast as each other when they're at full
speed. They both can run about 37 miles per hour.

FACT

Hyenas were kept as
pets and also raised
for food in Ancient
Egypt.

Another thing that wolves and hyenas have in common is that they're
intelligent and highly social animals. They hunt or at least find food in
groups. They also raise their cubs in dens. Groups of grey wolves are called
packs and groups of spotted hyenas are called clans. Hyena clans tend to be
larger than wolf packs and can have as many as eighty hyenas. A typical
wolf pack is usually about five to eleven wolves, though packs can join up
in a hunt. Wolves are also monogamous and the pack is led by an alpha

male and female. Most of the other pack members are their children. Male and female hyenas don't pair up in the same way. Hyenas also tend to be more aggressive toward their clan members in general. Male wolves help to raise their cubs, but male hyenas don't. Since they're so thoroughly dominated by the females they're probably too scared to try.

Also, if two hyena cubs of the same sex are born they will try to kill each other. This isn't true for wolf cubs, even though they start to play fight when they're about three weeks old.

Polar Bear V's Kodiak Bear

Battle of The Bears

If a polar bear and a Kodiak bear were to engage in combat, who would the winner be? Since both bears are massive in size, can be extremely aggressive, and possess the same types of "weapons," the outcome isn't obvious. First, let's consider each animal:

FACT

Polar bears have an excellent sense of smell. They can detect seals nearly a mile away just by sniffing the air.

Polar bears are easily recognizable because of their white fur. They live in the regions around the Arctic Circle, or North Pole. Although they spend most of their time on a solid ground of snow and ice, they also swim a great deal in the surrounding waters, either travelling between ice floes or searching for food, and their stamina is so great that they can swim up to 60 miles without stopping.

Polar bears are the largest of the bear species - adult males typically weigh between 775 and 1400 pounds. They also have very big paws that can measure up to a 12 inches across. Their claws are curved, thick, and very sharp, and they average around 3 inches in length. Polar bears can stand as high as 11 or 12 feet. They are fierce predators and, because of their size, have no real enemies in their normal environment.

These bears are carnivores, or meat-eaters, and they have 42 teeth which are also very sharp and allow them to rip and tear flesh. In fact, they are the largest land-dwelling carnivores on the planet.

Second in size to the polar bear is the great Kodiak bear, which gets its name from the Kodiak Archipelago, a small group of islands off the coast of Alaska where it lives. It is the largest of the brown bears, and males can weigh up to 1200 hundred pounds and stand as high as 10 feet tall.

FACT

The standard method of evaluating the size of bears is by measuring their skulls

Kodiak bears also have large paws with claws that can grow close to 6 inches long. Because of their habitat, Kodiak bears, unlike polar bears, are omnivorous, which means that they eat both meat and vegetation. However, the meat Kodiak bears consume is typically from smaller animals than those the polar bear feeds on.

So, if a polar bear and Kodiak bear were to take each other on in battle, who would win the fight?

Both bears will bring their "A-game," throwing their considerable weight and strength into the match. Each will employ teeth and claws in an attempt to wound its opponent into retreat or death.

However, as the bears lunge toward one another in attack, chances are great that the polar bear will ultimately be victorious due to the fact that it is typically the larger of the two animals and can use its sharper teeth and claws and more aggressive nature to its advantage.

Lappet Faced Vulture V's Bald Eagle

Instead of just telling you about the outcome of an airborne battle between a mighty bald eagle and a lappet faced vulture, which are both raptors of around the same size and weight, let's go live to the wilderness of the scorched plains and valleys to watch a fight as it happens.

Desert Scrap

A friendly breeze fluttered across the scrubby floor of the valley, ruffling the feathers of the vulture where he perched in the dead tree. He shifted his large shoulders and turned his head to scan the Eastern sky. His empty stomach twisted and he half-raised his wings and shuffled his feet along the dry branch.

FACT
The lappet-faced vulture is one of Africa's most aggressive birds.

He had been lurking here too long, unable to decide his next course of action. The Eagle's nest on the cliff behind him was unprotected, and one of the large eggs would settle his raging hunger. Stretching his wide wings, he swayed for a moment on the branch, before he rose lazily in the air.

He landed lightly beside the nest and craned his neck to blink at the clutch of eggs. This eagle's mate had died, and the scarcity of game had forced the female to go on an extended hunting break, ranging far from her unborn young. He considered the eggs, his curved beak opening slightly.

A sudden savage cry rose on the wind and his reaction was instantaneous. Lifting in the air he desperately tried to gain altitude, but his long, wide wings were not designed for rapid acceleration.

The screaming cry came again, as the large female bald eagle streaked for him, plummeting out of the sun. Instinctively, his stomach retched and tried to rid himself of any excess weight, but his system had been empty for days and he had nothing to vomit.

FACT

Bald Eagles are the national birds of the United States. Their nests can weigh as much as a ton!

Within seconds, she crashed into him, her piercing talons grasping his shoulders, cutting through feather and flesh. Her solid, feathery weight knocked him out of the air and he went spinning towards the rocks. Her talons ripped free from his shoulder and he felt heat and agony surging through him. He began flapping, desperately trying to regain his balance in the air.

The eagle dove mercilessly again. Blinking desperately, beak hanging open, he tried to get his left wing to stabilize, but the muscles were mangled from the grip of the eagle's powerful talons and he could feel blood dripping down his feathers on that side.

In a second, she was on him. As her claws closed on his back once more, he let himself go limp.

For a moment the eagle struggled under their combined weights, and then they began to plummet towards the dusty land below. The eagle's talons smoothly unclenched and with a mighty beat of her wings and a final cry she headed back towards her eggs.

Relieved, the vulture immediately set off on a hasty course away from the eagle's nest. He knew of a watering hole where he could rest and let his shoulder heal.

So there you have it. In a battle between a bald eagle and a lappet faced vulture, the winner every single time would be the mighty bald eagle.

Crocodile V's Hippopotamus

In African Waters

Every day, animals compete for survival, even the fiercest predators. Hippo's and crocodiles rarely get into quarrels, but that doesn't mean that it hasn't occurred. In a fight, who do you think would win? Do you think the hippo would win? What about the crocodile? Well, keep reading to discover the answer.

FACT

Crocodiles release heat through their mouths rather than through sweat glands!

Crocodile: These scary beasts are built to kill with their mega-sharp teeth, strong jaws and their ability to stay underwater for hours. Crocodiles have really thick skin that helps protect them from attacks from other animals. Their diet consists of fish, reptiles, birds and small mammals.

The death roll is a technique a croc' uses to kill its prey. Once it latches on to an arm, leg or body part, the crocodile begins to roll until the body part comes off. However, the crocodile's biggest asset is its jaw pressure. A typical crocodile's jaw pressure is around 23,100 psi.

Surprisingly, crocodiles are somewhat fast, despite their tiny legs and heavy body. They can run 10 to 13 miles per hour on land. In the water, a crocodile can swim up to 18 miles per hour.

Hippopotamus: Hippo's are the third largest mammal in Africa. Although they have short, stubby legs and a bulky body, hippos are quite fast. Some have been clocked to reach speeds of 30mph; that's as fast as a car going at medium speed.

FACT

Hippo's might look a bit flabby, but they can easily outrun a human.

Hippo's are cute, but don't be fooled by their appearance because they are one of the most dangerous animals in the world. Their jaws are very large, and they are strong enough to cut a human's body in half. In fact, most predatory animals try to stay as far away from a family of hippos as possible.

To stay cool under the hot African sun, hippo's stay in the water. Hippo's are feared by most predatory animals, but they do have to worry about attacks from lions and the occasional crocodile.

Who would win a fight between a crocodile and a hippo? Although they rarely get into quarrels, hippos and crocodiles have fought before. In a fair fight, a hippo would win.

Why? Hippo's would win a fight because they are larger, making it almost impossible for a crocodile to take one down. An adult hippo is extremely heavy, weighing in at an astonishing 2,600 lbs. On top of that, a crocodile is no match for the size a brute force of a hippo's jaw. However, a crocodile can inflict major battle scars on the hippo, but that isn't enough to win a fight.

Lion V's Grizzly Bear

Clash of Kings

In a fight between a lion and a grizzly bear, who would the winner be? Although, in the wild, these two animals live in completely different regions of the globe, the question is still a fun and interesting one to ponder. Lion V's grizzly - let's look at the facts:

Adult male lions are mighty and ferocious creatures. They are the main defenders of their habitat, which is located primarily on the plains of sub-Saharan Africa, and so are accustomed to battling other animals in order to keep what is theirs. They are the second-largest cat on the planet - the tiger is bigger overall - but they are the tallest when it comes to shoulder height. Males weigh, on average, between 350 and 550 pounds. Lions are carnivores, or meat-eaters, and have 30 teeth, including canine teeth that can be 3 inches long and enable them to grasp their prey and tear its flesh. Their jaws are very strong and allow the lion to grab and hold with great pressure. Lion claws are also long and very sharp and are attached to large, powerful paws. Only male lions have manes, a feature which makes them appear bigger and more imposing to their enemies. The lion can emit a thunderous roar that lets any opponent know it's time to back off or face the consequences.

Although the lion is an intimidating creature, the grizzly bear is also a formidable foe. The grizzly is a type of brown bear that lives mainly in the northwestern parts of the continental United States, western Canada, and Alaska. Standing as high as 10 feet tall, an adult male grizzly can weigh more than 800 pounds.

Like lions, grizzly bears have very sharp teeth, and their claws can be 3-5 inches long. Although these bears are omnivores, with a diet that includes vegetation such as nuts and berries, they are also deadly predators that will eat animals as large as moose. Known for their fierceness when confronted, grizzlies are masters of their territory, and any animal that comes up against one is in for a real battle.

FACT

Grizzly bears are usualy brown, but their fur can appear to be white-tipped, or grizzled, which is where they get their name.

So, in a brawl between the mighty lion and the massive grizzly, who would walk away the winner?

While both opponents possess similar weapons - sharp teeth and claws and a highly aggressive nature if confronted - when push comes to shove, it is the grizzly who will come out on top due to its size and strength. The lion may be king in its own land, but it is no match for the taller, heavier, and stronger grizzly, who towers over the lion when standing and can deliver a battle-ending blow with one of its massive paws.

African Elephant V's Rhinoceros

The Ultimate Showdown

FACT

Elephants can swim!
They use their trunk
to breathe like a snorkel
in deep water.

In a battle between the African Elephant and the rhinoceros, who would the ultimate victor be?

While the elephant is both bigger and taller than the rhino, each animal possesses certain traits that give it advantages when it comes to fighting.

The African Elephant does have size on its side. In fact, it is the world's biggest land animal, and males can stand as tall as 13 feet and weigh up to 8 tons. This makes the elephant a very strong creature.

The elephant's trunk, which is used for smelling, breathing, drinking, bathing, making calls, and grabbing things, can also be used as a weapon to easily throw, strike, or knock over objects in its path.

Its sharp tusks, which can grow up to 10 feet in length and are used to dig for food and water, strip bark, and move objects about, can also function as weapons. Each tusk has a tip that can work like a blade to allow the elephant to stab its enemy.

The elephant can use its large feet and height advantage to stomp anything beneath it. And because the elephant is one of the most intelligent animals on Earth, it can bring more brain power to a fight than the average rhinoceros.

However, the rhino is no weakling.

Although it is smaller than the African Elephant - males can weigh up to 2-3 tons and stand nearly 6 feet tall - it is still a very impressive creature that can use its physical force to intimidate and overpower its foes.

The rhino also has a horn, which it sharpens on rocks and trees. This horn can grow up to 4 feet long and can be used, like an elephant's tusk, to wound or kill whatever animal it comes up against.

In addition, the rhinoceros can run up to 35 miles per hour, which is 10 miles faster than the average elephant.

So who would win in a showdown between these two mighty beasts? As the elephant and rhino charge one another, each running as fast as it can towards its opponent in order to meet it with as much force as possible, the size and strength of the elephant will be too much for the rhino.

FACT

The name rhinoceros means 'nose horn' and is often shortened to rhino.

Both animals will also attempt to use their "blade", either tusk or horn, to injure the other. However, it will be difficult for the rhino to do mortal damage to the elephant because it is shorter and cannot reach the elephant's vital organs easily. And since the elephant is smarter and bigger overall, it will be able to sense the rhino's moves and answer them with more skill and power.

So, in this epic battle, the elephant is the winner!

Alligator V's Crocodile

Clash of the Reptiles

Picture the scene...

An alligator wades through the marsh, using its muscular tail to push it through the freshwater. Alligators do not have a functioning salt gland and are confined to living in ponds, rivers, and other salt-free bodies of water. Even though crocodiles do have a working salt gland and can live in saltwater, a small croc' has just wandered into freshwater territory and has begun stalking our alligator.

FACT

Alligator eggs become male or female alligators depending on the temperature!

On average, an alligator is smaller than a full grown crocodile. Because a standard crocodile is 5.8 meters long, and an average gator is 4.3 meters long, this small crocodile is an even match for our unaware alligator

Crocodiles usually ambush their prey. They wait for an animal to come to the edge of the water, or swim above them before they attack. Although crocodiles are very successful hunters, alligators have keen senses. The alligator we are watching has just used its impeccable hearing to detect the location of our trespassing crocodile and is now on the defense.

Alligators and crocodiles have many similar characteristics. B
at a speed of around 20mph and have a land speed that tops
Our alligator and crocodile both have eyes that are located forwaru
head, allowing them to judge distance extremely accurately.

The alligator and crocodile are aware of their similarities as they go into battle. Because both reptiles have been at the top of the food chain for the last 200 million years, it is difficult to predict the outcome of this impending fight.

The crocodile, being the more aggressive of the two animals, strikes first. Although its cover has been blown and it can no longer ambush the alligator, it uses its muscular body to lunge at its enemy. The alligator, agile and at home in the water, dodges the attack.

FACT

Crocodiles have the strongest bite of any animal in the world.

Crocodiles are hostile animals, but they become easily discouraged if they do not capture their prey on the first attempt. Our crocodile attempts to ambush the alligator one final time, but finds its neck caught in the U-shaped jaws of the enemy gator. The crocodile fights back, thrashing its strong body and biting at the gator with its V-shaped mouth.

A fight between an alligator and a crocodile would be an intense, but fast battle. Both reptiles are exceptional predators, built to quickly kill.

So what is the outcome of the skirmish? Well, even though crocodiles have been seen preying on lions that venture too close to the water's edge, without the element of surprise, the alligator's broader jaws would win this battle.

Why? Although both reptiles are extremely similar, the broad jaws of an alligator give its bite more surface area than a crocodile. This is the slight advantage that the gator needs to cause damage and defeat the crocodile.

Lion V's Tiger

Battle of the Big Cats

Throughout history, the lion and tiger have been admired by many for their strength, stamina, intelligence, and beauty.

These great cats are both fascinating and dangerous, and many have wondered, "If a lion and a tiger were fighting each other, who would win?" There are many factors to consider, as each cat has different defences and different ways of fighting.

FACT
The roar of a lion can be heard from 5 miles away!

The lion has some advantages over the tiger; he has a thick mane around his neck, that helps protect him in a fight. The lion lives in a group, called a pride, and has been raised with other lions and has been taught to fight since he was cub. He starts out learning to battle while play-fighting, and eventually the other lions will teach him to fight for real.

From the time the tiger is born, until he is two years old, he only lives with his mother, so he doesn't get lessons in fighting like the lion. But, the tiger does have some advantages that the lion doesn't have. The tiger, because he does not fight with other tigers, learns to fight alone and has his own special way of fighting which is very different from the lion. The tiger, who almost always has a larger body, stands up on his back legs when he fights. And because the tiger weighs more, he may be able to easily overcome the lion.

FACT
Tigers are good swimmers and can swim over 3 miles.

Both the lion and tiger have some of the same "weapons" given to them by Mother Nature. They both have powerful, muscular bodies. Their great paws help them to run quickly, and their claws are extremely sharp for cutting through flesh. They both have very sharp teeth and powerful jaws for biting down and holding on to their enemies. Both of these great cats, when they get into a fight, almost always never back down until one seriously injures the other. Fights between lions and tigers have been known to go on for up to an hour.

It's important to remember that even though each one of these great cats are efficient and have deadly ways to fight, they can also get hurt. If one of them receives a slash against his face by the other, he could lose an eye, have a serious injury across his nose, even get a bad cut on his mouth. When giant cats fight, they are usually in the wild, and if they get hurt, there is no one to take care of them. A slow painful death often follows a fight in the wild.

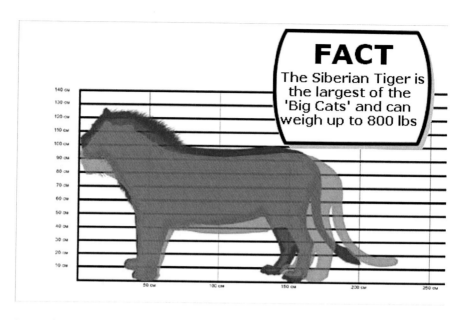

FACT
The Siberian Tiger is the largest of the 'Big Cats' and can weigh up to 800 lbs

In ancient times, when the Romans brought lions and tigers together for fighting, records have shown that the tiger almost always won over the lion.

Today, it's not uncommon for lions and tigers to fight with each other in captivity, when they do, and both of these magnificent animals are around the same size, the tiger will inevitably be victorious.

A Final Word

Thank you for reading 'When Deadly Creatures Fight – Who Would Win' if you liked it please would you do me a big favor and leave a review.

Thank you

Brian Good...

ABOUT THE AUTHOR

Brian Good began his career as a primary school teacher in Birmingham, United Kingdom. As his career progressed to Headteacher, LEA and OFSTED inspector, he developed an interest in early intervention techniques.

He spent some time teaching in Brisbane, Australia whilst continuing to work on creating strategies for the delivery of early years services and making the whole learning experience suitable for all children, at all times.

He is now a chartered educational psychologist and independent consultant advising schools across Sweden.

He has spent the last four years living with his wife of 31 years, Trudi and their beautiful Afghan hounds, Kysa and Malin in Halland, Sweden

Brian Good

For more information about this and other books that you may find interesting or to be updated when we release a new book please visit
Grey Whale Publishing.

www.greywhalepublishing.com

Brian Good

Made in the USA
San Bernardino, CA
04 December 2016